£1.00

ANNIE MILLER was a co-founder in 1984 of the charity that is now the Citizen's Basic Income Trust, and has been its Chair since 2001. She was also a co-founding member of the Basic Income European/Earth Network in 1986. She first became interested in Basic Income (BI) as a direct result of her experience of being treated as a second-class citizen by the UK's income tax and social security systems. She is convinced that a full BI, more than any other income maintenance system, can help to bring about emancipation, wellbeing and justice. A retired academic economist, :

By the same author:

A Basic Income Handbook, I
A Basic Income Pocketbook.

GW00400296

This book is not really designed to persuade the unpersuaded of the attractiveness of basic income... Instead, this book provides a framework for activists that clarifies what a basic income is, what it is not, what questions remain open for testing and where local discretion, debate and detailed thinking are still required. It helps us get our arguments straight and it stops us falling into some of the elephant traps that are waiting for us.

One of the great strengths of this book... is that she provides a very useful overview of all the different 'complexities' that are hidden within this seemingly simple idea.

  —*Multiple sources of possible funds for a basic income*
  —*Different models of basic income*
  —*Different levels of basic income*
  —*Various pathways to implementing basic income*
  —*Conditions that will need to exist to support basic income.*
      Simon Duffy, Centre for Welfare Reform

The very nature of work will change. The governments may have to consider stronger social safety nets and eventually Universal Basic Income.
António Guterres, UN Secretary General, 25 September 2018, at the General Assembly of the UN

This may be the time to consider a universal salary.
Pope Francis, Easter Monday, 13 April 2020 (see page 54)

[Some people] have suggested a minimum income, a guaranteed income for people. Is that worthy of attention now? Perhaps so.
Nancy Pelosi, Speaker of the United States House of Representatives

Universal income will be necessary over time if AI takes over most human jobs.
Elon Musk, founder and CEO of Spacex, CEO of Tesla, Inc., founder of The Boring Company, co-founder of Neuralink and co-founder OpenAI

All royalties generated from sales of this book will be donated to the Basic Income Earth Network (BIEN), Charity No. 1177066 www.basicincome.org.

The statements and opinions contained within this publication are solely those of the author, and do not necessarily express the views of any specific basic income organisation.

Essentials
of Basic Income

ANNIE MILLER

Luath Press Limited

EDINBURGH

www.luath.co.uk

First published 2020

ISBN: 978-1-913025-58-8

This book is made of material from well-managed,
FSC®-certified forests and other controlled sources.

Printed and bound by
Ashford Colour Press, Gosport

Typeset in 10.5 point Sabon by Main Point Books, Edinburgh

Contents

The Basic Income Earth Network's Definition of Basic Income

A **basic income** is a periodic cash payment unconditionally delivered to all on an individual basis, without means test or work requirement.

That is, basic income has the following **five characteristics**:

1. **Periodic:** it is paid at regular intervals (for example every month), not as a one-off grant.

2. **Cash payment:** it is paid in an appropriate medium of exchange, allowing those who receive it to decide what they spend it on. It is not, therefore, paid either in kind (such as food or services) or in vouchers dedicated to a specific use.

3. **Individual:** it is paid on an individual basis – and not, for instance, to households.

4. **Universal:** it is paid to all, without means test.

5. **Unconditional:** it is paid without a requirement to work or to demonstrate willingness-to-work.

www.basicincome.org/basic-income

A basic income model compared with an income tax schedule.

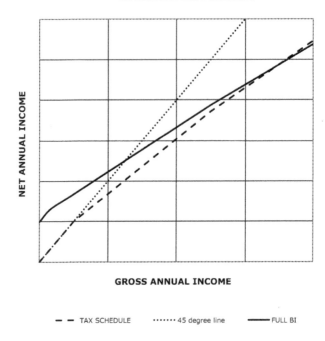

NET ANNUAL INCOME

GROSS ANNUAL INCOME

— — TAX SCHEDULE   ⋯⋯ 45 degree line   —— FULL BI

The diagram compares the effects on net income of an income tax schedule with that of a BI scheme and its associated income tax system. It shows that the basic income provides greatest advantage for low-income people and this reduces as gross income increases, and is likely to become negative for high income earners. (The 45-degree line represents the effect on net income when there are no taxes or transfers.)

Introduction

GLOBAL INTEREST IN basic income (BI) has increased enormously in recent years, with the failure of many national social protection systems and the successful BI experiments in both India and Finland fuelling speculation as to its worldwide applicability. The concept is deceptively simple and difficult to define. The international educational charity, Basic Income Earth Network (BIEN) provides the first port of call for information about basic income.

BIEN's definition of a BI on its website, revised in 2016, comprises an explanatory sentence (as defined in its constitution) accompanied by a commentary on the five characteristics that expand the idea. However, the commentary needs some clarification and is inadequate for distinguishing between BI and related concepts, such as a negative income tax (NIT) or a means-tested benefit (MTB), for academic purposes.

In BIEN's commentary, the characteristic 'Universal' states that 'it is paid to all', but it could be interpreted as also being 'unconditional' in the sense that everyone receives the same amount. This interpretation can also be confused with the characteristic 'Unconditional'. These confusions can be reduced by adding a sixth characteristic, 'Uniform'.

Maybe some BI advocates assume that a BI would be uniform (except that it could vary by age). But there is nothing in the BIEN definition or commentary that requires it to be so. Many would be appalled if a BI scheme proposed paying different amounts to men and women and yet it could still be categorised as a BI scheme under the current BIEN definition.

On pages 19–20 some related concepts are defined, not in order to reject them, since they can serve useful purposes, but to enable more precise discussions to take place.

One objective of this book is to offer clarification of various issues, for discussion by members of BIEN.

A second aim is to explore the implications of a more academic definition of the generic basic income. These include some justifications for a BI on ethical, social and economic grounds, and the direct effects of a BI system upon society. It is by exploring these implications that its potential benefits are most acutely expressed.

The six revised characteristics of basic income define a class of income maintenance systems within which a wide variety of BI schemes or models is possible. Thus, a third aim is to provide a clear, concise, accurate and comprehensive account of the essentials of BI which separates the generic BI from matters that rightly belong to the domain of proposals for, or the implementation of, BI schemes and models.

This book seeks not only to inform but to inspire and encourage others in the fight for an equal, compassionate society. The implementation of a basic income will not immediately ameliorate the suffering and injustices that so many of our fellow citizens encounter in their day-to-day lives, but it is a necessary step if we are to move in the right direction.

However, the BI debate has been overtaken by events. The onset of the Covid-19 pandemic early in 2020 has presented the strongest case yet for basic income schemes across the world, together with a world-wide system to help poorer countries. The fight for compassion and justice is even more urgent now than ever.

1

The Inadequacies of Social Insurance and Social Assistance Systems

A WELFARE STATE comprises public welfare services and a social security system, which is divided into a contributory social insurance (SI) system and a mainly means-tested social assistance (SA) safety-net.

Contributory SI systems are inadequate as social protection mechanisms. They aim to provide *income-replacements* for employees when they are unable to earn a living due to circumstances beyond their control, such as sickness, unemployment or retirement.

However, the coverage of a social insurance scheme can be incomplete, because:

- It covers only people who are in paid work

- The delivery unit is the individual employee

- The amount of the insurance benefit is based on the individual's contribution record.
  Insurance benefits may be augmented to cover some of the costs of the employee's financial dependents.

The employee is expected to remain in paid work until pension-entitlement age, unless prevented by circumstances beyond his/her control.

Gaps in an employee's contribution record can lead to reduced benefits. However, some 'economically inactive' people, including many unpaid carers (mainly women) of children, elders and others, are unable to build up their contribution records towards their own pensions, let alone receive unemployment or sickness benefits. Nor do self-employed people usually enjoy the same protection as employees.

An SI system works best for jurisdictions with well-educated populations, in full employment, with state-funded childcare provision staffed by highly qualified nursery staff and where nearly everyone is in well-paid, full-time, secure employment over a lifetime.

Those who are not eligible for SI benefits may be able to apply for means-tested SA. Often involving below-subsistence benefits, SA also suffers from major structural faults:

1. The delivery unit is usually the cohabiting couple (married or otherwise), requiring a joint application for benefits. Thus, the poorer partner of a couple may be trapped in the role of 'financial dependent', at risk of economic abuse, and with no independent source of income with which to feed herself and her children.

2. Means-tested benefits (MTBs) are targeted at low income people, but it does not necessarily protect them. Rather, it can segregate and stigmatise, humiliate and reject them, leading to low take-up of the benefits to which they are entitled.

3. MTBs often involve making extra deductions from earnings in addition to taxes on income, which can create a higher effective-income-tax rate and introduce an inherent disincentive to work-for-pay for claimants.

4. Receipt of their benefits is usually conditional on claimants fulfilling behavioural requirements, and non-compliance can lead to sanctions, all of which can create stress and anxiety.

However, when the flaws in the social assistance system have been addressed and corrected, a BI emerges.

2

The Generic Basic Income:
A Proposed Clarification

BIEN's DEFINITION OF the generic basic income, as quoted above, is accurate as far as it goes, but it needs further clarification and is inadequate for distinguishing a BI from other related concepts. The characteristic 'Uniform' must be introduced, having been disentangled from its close associations with both 'Universal' and 'Unconditional'. Therefore, a revision is presented here that offers greater clarity.

(Words in italics on pages 16–22 have been changed from, or added to, the BIEN definition at: www.basicincome.org/basic-income/.)

A **basic income** is a periodic cash payment unconditionally delivered to all on an individual basis, without means test or work requirement.

That is, basic income has *six* characteristics:

It is periodic, a cash payment, individual-based, universal, uniform (except by age) and unconditional.

These six characteristics are defined as follows:

1. **Periodic**: it is paid *at the beginning of the period to which it relates,* at regular intervals (for example every month), not as a one-off grant.

2. **Cash payment:** it is paid in an appropriate medium of exchange, allowing those who receive it to decide what they spend it on. It is not, therefore, paid either in kind (such as food or services) or in vouchers dedicated to a specific use. *It is paid gross, that is, without any personal tax or other deductions.*

3. **Individual:** it is *delivered* on an individual basis – and not, for instance, *on the basis of a couple or* household.

4. **Universal:** *this indicates who is eligible.* It is paid to all, *including to a child to be administered on her/his behalf by the primary care-giving parent or another registered responsible person. It is not targeted at particular sections of the population according to specific categories or circumstances, such as an occupation group or low-income people.*

5. *Uniform: the amount of a basic income is the same/equal for everyone within a given territorially-defined jurisdiction at a given time, except that it could vary by age, but not according to specific categories or circumstances, such as those based on personal attributes, household living arrangements, employment status, insurance contribution record, income, wealth or worth.*

6. **Unconditional:** *a basic income is not conditional on the recipient having to fulfil any behavioural requirements, such as participating*

in authorised activities. It is paid without a requirement to work or to demonstrate willingness-to-work, *to undertake volunteer work, or to behave according to traditional gender roles. In other words, it is* **obligation-free.**

The term 'basic' refers to the fact that it is a foundational income upon which each person can build with income from other sources.

3

Related Concepts

IT WOULD BE helpful if definitions of some related concepts could be included on the BIEN website such as the following:

Basic Income (BI) and its related concepts form a family of cash transfer programmes. The related concepts could perform useful roles during the transition process towards a comprehensive BI system. The revised definition set out above helps to distinguish the generic BI from its related concepts for academic purposes.

*A **basic endowment** is a one-off grant paid to all, that could be delivered at the start of adult life. It fails characteristic 1.*

***Negative income tax** (NIT): an NIT is the result of the integration of an income tax system and a grant-awarding programme. But not all NITs incorporate the characteristics of a BI. Even where an NIT appears to resemble a BI system, there are still perceivable differences. For example, if financed, at least in part, by taxes on personal income, a BI scheme and its associated, individual-based, income tax system could be converted into an NIT. The essential difference between them is mainly administrative. A BI is paid in advance and separately from the income* tax payments. The NIT is a combination of a payment and a tax on income, and typically the transaction is made in arrears of the period to which the benefit relates. However, an NIT is also divisive, effectively targeting the poorest, since its cash transfer system distinguishes between those who receive a net payment and those who are net taxpayers. An NIT fails characteristics 1, 2 and 4.

A **tax credit** (TC) system would allow the BI payment to be used to reduce the tax liability of the individual. It fails characteristics 1 and 2.

A **targeted income** would be paid only to particular sections of the population according to specific categories or circumstances. It fails characteristic 4.

A **means-tested benefit** (MTB) results from the combination of targeting low-income people and reducing their payments as their means (their gross income and/or wealth) increase (in addition to deducting taxes on income), until the benefit has effectively been withdrawn. MTBs fail characteristics 4 and 5.

A **minimum income guarantee** (MIG) is a type of MTB with the payment being reduced at the rate of 100 per cent as gross income increases. It fails characteristics 4 and 5.

A **participation income** (PI) could be similar to a BI, except that it imposes behavioural requirements on recipients. It fails characteristic 6.

BIEN's definition on its website is followed by a passage that implicitly limits the extent of the definition, and then also makes the important distinction between full and partial BIs:

> A wide variety of Basic Income proposals are circulating today. They differ along many other dimensions, including in the amounts of the Basic Income, the source of funding, the nature and size of reductions in other transfers that might accompany it, and so on.
>
> BIEN is a charitable organisation dedicated to taking an educational role, and therefore, it cannot endorse any particular proposal...
>
> A Basic Income that is stable in size and frequency and high enough to be, in combination with other social services, part of a policy strategy to eliminate material poverty and enable the social and cultural participation of every individual is often called a 'full Basic Income', and a lower one is often called a 'partial Basic Income'. *In either case of 'full' or 'partial' Basic Income, its introduction would not replace social services or entitlements, if that replacement worsens the situation of relatively disadvantaged, vulnerable or lower-income people.* However, the definitions of 'full' and 'partial' are highly controversial, and BIEN has not attempted to define them officially.
>
> ...

A permanent system, providing a BI over a lifetime, could ensure a regular, reliable, predictable source of income. It is important that the level of the BI should be stable over time and protected from sudden declines or erosion in real terms.

Constitutional safeguards will be required, to prevent later administrations from overturning a Basic Income system summarily. Also, the right to a Basic Income should be guaranteed by constitution, and not withdrawn from anyone who meets the eligibility criteria, except in the most extreme of circumstances, and then only by a country's parliament or highest court. Protective legislation would be needed to prevent Basic Incomes from being used as security for loans, or mortgages, which could lead to negative equity and deprive the recipients of their future income streams and put them at risk of permanent destitution. A Basic Income must be inalienable, that is, protected from sequestration (debt collection procedures).

4

Counter Arguments to Common Criticisms of BI

If the unit for delivery is the individual, and the payment is uniform, will this not lead to advantages for shared households, due to economies of scale?

If it is important to minimise that advantage, then all shared households and multiple-occupancy accommodation would have to be treated in the same way. Even if this were desirable, it would not be practical.

The unit for delivery being the individual frees the poorer partner in a relationship from the 'financial dependence' trap, and potential economic abuse.

Different levels of payment for partners and for single people require continual intrusive monitoring of relationships.

Often, couples (married, in civil partnerships or otherwise co-habiting) are discriminated against when assessed for benefits, whereas other adults sharing accommodation, such as two siblings, or an older adult with grown-up offspring, are not.

Household economies of scale provide an incentive for people to share accommodation (including the parents of dependent children who want to stay together), and could also reduce the demand for single adult housing.

Why give it to rich people who do not need it?

In order to create a just, united and *inclusive* society, everyone must receive a BI.

Rich people tend to value a universal system from which they benefit, and thus will protect it more effectively for the most vulnerable in society, compared with targeted benefits.

It is more administratively efficient (cheaper) to ensure that everyone has a BI and to assess individuals' incomes for income or other tax just once a year, rather than assessing them a second time for means-tested benefits.

A progressive income tax, or a wealth tax, could ensure that the wealthiest do not profit overall from the introduction of a BI system.

Why give something for nothing? What about reciprocity?

A BI is not 'something for nothing'. It is based on people's rights to a share of their nation's natural resources and material heritage.

Thomas Paine wrote about the land and natural resources belonging to the people, and where it has been appropriated for private use, those owners owe a ground rent to the whole excluded population. (Paine, *Agrarian Justice*, 1796).

The wealth of a nation is built on the infrastructure

and material heritage of previous generations. It is also derived from the intangible capital and the quality of its institutions, especially the rule of law. The wealthier the nation, the more this is so. The BI can be regarded as a dividend from the economy, which is underpinned by this heritage.

The first duty of any government is to guarantee the security of its people – starting with their income security, as provided by a BI. This is also an economic investment in the population.

A BI should not be conditional on reciprocity. The right to life, and to be not destitute, should be sacrosanct. Otherwise people die prematurely for the 'crime' of being poor.

In a healthy society, most people will act responsibly and with charity. Reciprocity is a two-way exchange, and who is to say from which direction it should come first? Acts of generosity often invoke corresponding feelings of gratitude and generosity in the recipient, such that they feel moved to respond and contribute to society later, in a manner that is meaningful to them. Many who might formerly have been regarded as 'undeserving' could be transformed and revealed as 'deserving'.

As Adam Smith wrote in *The Wealth of Nations*, 1776:

> Is this improvement in the circumstances of the lower rank of the people to be regarded as an advantage or as an inconvenience to the society? The answer seems at first sight abundantly plain.

Servants, labourers and workmen of different kinds, make up the far greater part of every political society. But what improves the circumstances of the greater part can never be regarded as an inconveniency to the whole. No society can surely be flourishing and happy, of which the far greater part of the members are poor and miserable.

What if everyone gave up working for pay? What about free-riders?

Some people, for whom 'work is what gives meaning to life', want to make working for pay compulsory for all, although, if true, compulsion should not be necessary.

A partial BI would not be enough to live on, so there would certainly be incentives to work-for-pay. Even with a full BI, people would still want to earn and spend more.

All of the evidence indicates that people want to work-for-pay, not just for the earnings, but for the social and health advantages that employment offers – the chance to make friends, to have a structure to one's day or week, to develop one's skills, to take pride in doing socially useful work well, and to be acknowledged as someone who is contributing to the economy and society.

The financial security of a full BI, by reducing the risk of destitution, could enable self-employed people's companies, small businesses and worker co-operatives to grow, releasing creative enterprise.

Some people might want to reduce their hours of

paid work in order to achieve a better work/life balance, to spend more time on raising their children or elder care.

Some might prefer to use their BIs to pursue educational goals. Others might want to take an occasional sabbatical to travel, or to achieve some lifetime ambition.

Since a BI would not undermine the incentives to work for pay for most people, let us tolerate the few free-riders (whose lives are devoted to pure leisure) exercising their right to choose, and for whom the incentives are still not sufficient, as long as they do no harm. A BI weakens their critics' claims based on the work ethic, because everyone would be entitled to make this choice.

5

What Difference Could a BI Make?

EACH MAIN DEFINING characteristic of the generic BI could contribute directly to several related short-term and long-run objectives for welfare reform.

A full BI could lead to the following outcomes:

a) **Emancipation**: each person is respected and valued for her/his own sake. A BI bestows dignity, privacy and financial autonomy. By trusting adults with more control over the use of their own time, together with financial security, a BI emancipates and empowers them, increasing their life choices. No longer at other people's mercy, emancipation is worth far more than the monetary value of the benefit.

b) **Wellbeing**: a BI can help to prevent, or at least reduce, both the depth and incidence of income poverty (in terms of deprivation, stigma, uncertainty and exclusion). Providing financial security – granting the unconditional right not to be destitute – could help to reduce anxiety and chronic stress and thus improve both mental and physical health. Enabling parents to spend more time nurturing and socialising their children would be an investment in the emotional and social development of future generations. In the long run, a BI could increase wellbeing in terms of security, living standards, nutrition, health and educational opportunities, helping people to develop to their full potentials, and reducing demands on health and other personal services.

c) **A just and inclusive society**: a BI could help to redistribute income, from rich to poor, from men to women, and geographically. The flat rate of the BI would have a greater impact on those with no, low or fluctuating incomes than on those with high ones and could help to reduce personal debt. More choice over the use of one's own time could enable, among other things, civic engagement and local energy and food self-provisioning. It could foster community and social solidarity and help to heal our divided societies. Eventually, it could help to create a just, united and inclusive society. But, *income* inequalities could be reduced most effectively if the BI system were to be financed by a progressive *income tax* system.

d) **Labour market efficiency, flexibility and productivity**: economic theory recognises two incentives that influence the number of hours in a given period that a worker wishes to offer in any particular job (her/his labour supply) – unearned income, such as a BI, and the real net wage rate. A BI will have the greatest effect on those who are deprived of either leisure or income (those with the most elastic labour supply curves), potentially leading to a redistribution between those in paid and unpaid work, as people adjust their work/life balances.

It can be shown that the reservation wage (below which it is not worth working-for-pay) is inversely related to the BI level until the latter reaches subsistence level. Thus, a BI could make part-time work economically viable for low-wage earners. Similarly, non-means-testing of benefits restores the incentive to work-for-pay inherent in the net wage rate for claimants. A generous BI could enable employees to negotiate for fair pay, flexibility and good working conditions, or to refuse the worst jobs, depending on the labour market situation. A BI increases workplace democracy. More skills training and work choices could increase productivity.

e) **A relatively straightforward cash transfer administration system:** given that an individual fulfils the eligibility criteria, administration will involve registration, delivery, monitoring and compliance. Individualisation, universality, non-differentiation, and the non-conditionality of the BI system would require relatively simple administration, reducing the risk of fraud or error by either recipient or staff, and keeping administration costs to a minimum. It would not normally be intrusive into people's lives. It should also avoid the time-consuming personal effort and stress required of many claimants in order to apply for and retain means-tested benefits. Eventually it could lead to a more transparent and accountable administration system.

Obviously, BI is not about just one single issue, and the combination of equity, community, choice and efficiency goals appeals to those on both left and right of the political spectrum. The defining characteristics of the generic BI and the broad objectives to which they can contribute are interrelated (Miller, 2020: 54–55). All of the main characteristics are necessary to enable both men and women to experience the outcomes, of which financial security is probably the most important, in that it enables the full experience of the other outcomes. Even a partial BI could contribute towards these objectives, given the poverty of millions of people, living below subsistence levels in both rich and poor contries around the world. The more generous the BI, the more fully will these objectives be achieved.

The underlying question for any policy proposal must be: 'What sort of society do we want to create for ourselves and for future generations?' One based on the ideals of wisdom, justice, compassion and integrity would appeal to many people. BI's set of potential outcomes would appear to be key elements for *liberté*, *égalité* and *fraternité*.

Some institutions bring out the worst in people. Basic income seems to bring out the best in them – as evidenced by the Finnish experiment, where initial results indicated that recipients felt much happier, and the Indian experiment where the outcomes fell into three areas: an emancipatory effect, improvement in wellbeing and an increase in productivity. Some families, by pooling their BIs, were able to buy a family member out of bonded labour (Davala *et al*, 2015).

Some neoliberals have proposed a BI scheme in exchange for the dismantling of all public welfare services, in order to achieve 'low taxation'. In contrast, other people prefer Universal Basic Services (UBS) to a BI. But BI and UBS are complements, rather than substitutes, for each other. Some needs are better satisfied by a cash payment, for instance for food or clothing, while other needs are better served by public welfare services, such as health and education. However, they appear to be competing for the same funding resources.

A BI is not a panacea for all ills. BI is a necessary condition for a better society, but, by itself, is not sufficient to bring it about. It needs a range of other government policies on infrastructure and public services to fulfil the vision of a just, inclusive, peaceful society of fulfilled, emancipated individuals.

6

Who Would Benefit?

WOMEN COMPRISE THE largest single group of people who would benefit from a BI, particularly married women and those in civil partnerships or otherwise co-habiting, who would be released immediately from the financial dependence that traps so many of them, and, with it, the threat of economic or other abuse.

Having one's own unconditional source of income could emancipate and empower women. It could enable them to negotiate for a better allocation of domestic chores and caring responsibilities in the home. It could give them more control over major life choices, including leaving an abusive relationship or entering a new partnership, starting a family or having another child, moving to a larger house or downsizing, taking a job or starting a business.

Many people, both men and women, would like to help to care for close relatives and friends, especially ageing parents, but cannot afford to give up even part of their jobs in order to provide these services. A generous BI would give them the financial security to make that choice.

Some critics claim that receiving a BI would force women back into their kitchens. It is true that some women in low-paid, part-time, insecure, soul-destroying, drudge jobs might prefer to spend more time at home caring for children or elders, a privilege that many wealthier women already enjoy. But no-one is forcing them, and men will face the same choice.

However, the introduction of a BI scheme is also likely to affect men's lives. Many workers are aware that if they lost their jobs and were unable to find another one within two or three months, it could be followed by long-term unemployment, increased poverty, personal debt, the risk of losing their homes, marriages and families, and ultimately homelessness.

The guarantee of an income that could prevent destitution would reduce chronic stress levels and help to relieve other mental health symptoms. More men could have the option of choosing a more congenial work/life balance, and experience the joys and responsibilities of being involved in the daily care and upbringing of their children. Similarly, with a full BI, lone mothers and fathers and their children could lead fuller lives.

Young adults in late teenage years and early 20s comprise another group who could benefit from some financial independence, administering their own BIs and learning financial skills. They would benefit as students, when their BIs could contribute towards their maintenance costs, and later as young adults when starting out in life.

Writers and other artists would value the security

that a BI could give them while developing their creative talents and setting up their own businesses. It could also enable people to update their work skills regularly, and help life-long learning to become a reality.

Again, a partial BI could contribute towards these outcomes, but the more generous the BI, the greater its effects.

7

Designing a BI Scheme or Model

THE SIX REVISED characteristics of the generic basic income define a class of income maintenance systems within which a wide variety of BI schemes or models is possible. The process of translating theory into practice starts here.

Each jurisdiction presents different problems and constraints. Each will have a set of prioritised objectives for its BI scheme, tailored to meet its needs. Thus, even though each model could be based on the same genuine BI definition, the diverse contexts will lead to a variety of BI schemes.

Universality must be translated into **eligibility criteria**. Since 'citizenship' is a multi-faceted concept, involving political, civil, social and economic rights and responsibilities, it could be challenging to apply. However, many BI advocates recommend that eligibility be based on residency qualifications, such as the legal right to permanent residence in the jurisdiction, together with his/her main residence being located in it and being subject to its taxation laws. It could include the fulfilment of a period of legal and physical residency prior to receipt of the BI, and continuing physical residency for the major part of each year while receiving it.

The eligibility criteria will have to consider several categories of people, including those nationals of the jurisdiction who have chosen to work and live abroad but now want to return home, students on exchange schemes, travellers, homeless people, asylum seekers applying for refugee status and other migrants. Including provision for guest workers and migrants is especially important during the pandemic.

A worldwide BI system would be more effective than current foreign aid methods for providing opportunities in poorer countries, by satisfying the aspirations of those who might otherwise reluctantly decide to migrate and who could have contributed to their country's brain drains.

Each jurisdiction will have to decide at what age a child becomes an adult and can administer his/her own BI, and whether the amounts of the BI will vary by age. It will have to set up a system to register responsible adults to administer the BI on behalf of individuals with reduced mental capacity.

Jurisdictions that aspire to poverty-prevention levels of full BI could refer to official **poverty benchmarks**, such as that of the European Union, based on 60 per cent of the median equivalised household disposable income in each country. Equivalisation involves the application of weights to different household configurations, usually according to the ages of household members and other criteria, in order to make comparisons. Or the jurisdiction could merely index the BI to a proportion of GDP per capita.

However, the **implementation** of a comprehensive, full BI scheme all at once could be quite disruptive to an economy, although it would be less so during a recession or depression, such as during and after the Covid-19 pandemic. A cross-sectional approach, introducing a BI to different age groups in turn, would be possible. Alternatively, gradual implementation, by increasing partial BIs over time, could be quicker. Where partial BIs are concerned, a case might be made for differentiation of the amount in favour of some vulnerable groups, such as for lone parents (by giving the same enhanced BI to *all* primary care-giving parents, thus avoiding having to distinguish between lone and other parents, and also reducing household economies of scale for two-parent families).

Tax-exempt **disability benefits** to cover the extra costs incurred by disabled people, not just to survive with dignity, but in order to achieve their full potential, would be paid in a separate system to disabled people and their paid carers, in addition to BI.

If a BI contained a uniform element to cover **housing costs,** it would act as a powerful redistributive mechanism in favour of poorer areas within the country. But it is likely to be the poorer communities in expensive areas who would have to uproot from their familiar neighbourhoods and social support networks, now coveted by richer people. In jurisdictions with great variation in house prices and rents, a separate system for meeting housing needs and related costs may have to be retained or devised.

A BI should fulfil many of the same functions for which **contribution-based and means-tested benefits** were designed. It can smooth incomes during times of unemployment by providing a floor for those with no, low or variable earnings – including those who are unable to take on paid work, who are unemployable or unemployed, and the old, the sick and unpaid care-givers.

Jurisdictions will have to decide how to treat any existing contribution-based social insurance benefits, for instance whether basic state pensions (often with portability rights) will be replaced or enhanced by BIS.

Similarly, each jurisdiction will have to decide how to treat existing means-tested and other social assistance benefits. It would be advisable to retain any existing means-tested benefits (MTBS) until the BI system is fully implemented, to ensure that no claimants inadvertently become worse off. It is essential to protect the poorest people from financial losses during this process, or, better still, to improve their financial situations.

In order for poorer people to be better off financially, either the BI will have to be greater than the existing MTBS, or some or all of the BI will have to be disregarded, and only any remaining part treated as income when calculating entitlement to MTBS. The claimants would be floated off the MTBS as the amount of the BI increased over time.

As the BI levels increase, the MTB system will gradually wither away, eventually leaving only a residual system of benefits for which the BI is not a good substitute. New ways of accommodating the unanticipated needs that they served will be required. For instance, maternity benefits could be replaced by initiating the child BI (and a premium for a new mother) at, or back-dated to, the thirteenth week of pregnancy. Similarly, bereavement benefits could be replaced by continuing to pay the BI into the estate of the deceased for a period of time after death.

Ironically, a jurisdiction with a complex cash transfer system could find it more difficult to design a BI system to fit in with its existing one, than those with more rudimentary ones.

Good substitutes might not be available for other existing benefits, such as a fund for emergency payments in the event of fire or floods (increasing in frequency), and so these would have to be retained.

The initial implementation of a BI system will require good information, the setting up of individual bank accounts or smart cards, and a database of recipients' details. Subsequent administration will involve registration of births and deaths, and changes in individuals' contact details, the delivery of the BI, monitoring for continuing fulfilment of eligibility criteria, for fraud – including identity fraud – and for compliance.

8

Sources of Finance and Potential Savings

A BI SCHEME could be financed by either a single source or a combination of sources. Several potential funding sources have been proposed. Their suitability depends on one's objectives and the amount of revenue that a particular source could raise, as well as cultural norms.

If one wants to redistribute income from rich to poor people, then a **progressive income tax** system would be the most effective choice. Some jurisdictions are particularly averse to this type of taxation.

A wealth-holding tax, such as a **land value tax** (LVT), or annual ground rent, could also provide a method of redistributing wealth, especially relevant in countries with very unequal distributions of land- and property-holding. If a jurisdiction kept a reliable register of assets, then other types of wealth-holding might be taxed.

A **capital tax** on technology and equipment that displaces labour could be a source of finance for a BI, but it would require international co-operation to enforce it – as would the alternative of imposing dual public and private ownership in order to be able to distribute a universal economic dividend.

Corporation tax is a tax on the profits of companies and other enterprises. Competition between jurisdictions, offering the lowest rates of this tax to corporations who register their businesses in their territories, is leading to a race to the bottom, thus reducing the tax revenue raised.

A **sales tax** and a **value added tax** (VAT) are taxes on expenditure (which, in the absence of an income tax, would allow personal savings to be free from taxation). The difference between the two taxes is that any VAT that has been paid by VAT-registered businesses can be reclaimed from the tax authorities, whereas a sales tax cannot be reclaimed. Expenditure taxes tend to be regressive and a dampener on investment and jobs. But a sales tax on goods and services, including those sold by international companies, might partially compensate for the loss of corporation tax revenue legally avoided by these companies.

Taxes on the use of **scarce resources**, or on pollutants, such as **carbon taxes**, are increasingly essential but are designed to change behaviour, and if this is successful, it could have the unfortunate consequence of reducing the tax base and its revenue as a potential source of funding for a BI.

The **Tobin Financial Transaction Tax** was proposed originally to reduce speculation in currency deals. It could be widened to cover other financial transactions, but would probably require international co-operation to implement it. However, if each state kept a reliable register of financial transactions, it could charge a small rate of tax on each.

Sovereign Wealth Funds (SWFS) are based on community control of community-owned natural resources, such as land, water, clean air, minerals, forests, broadcast spectrum, real estate or beaches. Their revenues can be ring-fenced for designated purposes. Alaska and Norway set up SWFS in the 1970s based on oil revenues, which have been invested in the international stock market. They can help to protect inter-generational equity, but they are a long-term solution.

Seigniorage, or quantitative easing, refers to a government issuing extra currency to fund the BIS, thereby increasing the money supply. However, if carried out on a regular basis it would be inflationary, unless the surplus money was extracted from the economy equally regularly via some form of taxation. Besides, seigniorage has a much more important role to play in financing both physical and social infrastructures, which add to the wealth of, and therefore income for, society.

Savings might also be made, where both existing benefit systems and poverty-alleviation programmes are eventually replaced by a BI, or where the BI reduces the indirect costs of poverty on health and personal services, and on the criminal justice system. Administrative savings could also occur.

Many advocates propose abolishing or reducing any

income-tax-free allowance because this function would now be fulfilled by the BI. Complete abolition of the tax-free allowance would mean that every unit of gross income, even from the first, would have to be taxed. Retaining a small tax-free allowance would be beneficial both to taxation staff and to the public, who could avoid having to submit a tax return merely for casual earnings. It would also be more efficient for the BI to be exempt from taxes on income, rather than a larger BI being paid out, which would then be taxed.

The allowances, reliefs and exemptions in different tax systems lead to **legal tax avoidance**, reducing the tax base, and increasing the tax rates for those who cannot avoid paying the taxes. These 'tax welfare systems' can be very costly to a jurisdiction in terms of tax revenue foregone.

Similarly, **illegal tax evasion** also imposes burdens on other tax payers, which could more profitably be used to finance the BIs, if evasion could be reduced or eliminated.

9

We Can Afford It

THE KEY TO a politically expedient BI system is

- to provide adequate BIs that could meet the need of most individuals and reduce inequality, and

- to control costs to affordable, sustainable levels, while retaining incentives to work for pay.

The gross outlay on a BI system could be expensive. But, if it is financed by a progressive tax system, then it is merely transferring a smaller amount of income or wealth from rich to poor people, and will not be a dead weight loss on the economy. The distributive effects are far more important than the overall cost.

Some people object not only to the overall cost, but specifically to a rise in the rates of certain taxes, particularly income tax. And yet it could result in most of the population becoming financially better off than before, even more so with higher rates. Why then would the population object to higher income tax rates if a BI could make the majority of them better off? Taxation is the price of a good society. Financial gain or loss is only one of the factors that influence individuals in their choice of a system.

It is important to remember that a BI scheme is not about some people giving up part of their 'self-made income' to pay for less fortunate individuals. It is about societies worldwide making restitution to the dispossessed sections of their populations, who have been denied access to resources and live in poverty. It is about investment in the marginalised to enable them to transform their lives and develop to their full potentials.

Affordability is not necessarily about the size of the outlay or low levels of taxation, but value for money for the outcomes achieved by the BI system (that is, an investment in the people). This begs the question: can we afford *not* to implement a comprehensive BI system?

10

Some Economic Effects

A BI SYSTEM could help to regenerate areas of multiple deprivation. People in these areas will have less debt and more money in their pockets; demand will increase; new companies will move in, investing in the local area and workforce, and those who are confident enough might set up their own businesses.

BIs will give self-employed people, small businesses and workers' co-operatives the necessary financial security to grow their enterprises, releasing creative energies. A population receiving an adequate BI will provide a healthier workforce for business, with fewer days lost to absenteeism.

One of a government's roles is to raise taxes to pay for expenditure on behalf of the people – to pay the cost of both infrastructure and the provision of public welfare services. A different role is that of raising taxes to redistribute income and wealth, which is not a cost to the economy.

Redistribution from rich to poor, benefiting a very large number of poor people, will give an initial boost to the national economy, since poorer people have a greater propensity to consume, compared with affluent people who tend to save more or spend on imported luxuries. However, policies to foster only *sustainable* growth will be necessary.

If the BI system were financed out of taxation, as opposed to increasing the money supply as in quantitative easing, then it is not expected to be inflationary. However, wage adjustments and price changes would still occur. Wage rates for unpleasant labour could rise, and those of interesting, comfortable jobs are likely to fall. If the supply of a particular good (such as affordable housing) did not rise to meet increased demand, then its price could rise in the short term.

In the longer term, a comprehensive BI could lead to a lower national minimum wage, and employers might reduce their standard working week, or their wages (as will their competitors, competing away excess profits), enabling companies to trade more successfully.

Artificial intelligence (AI) and automation have already had a profound impact on labour forces around the world. It is still unknown whether it will continue at the same pace or how long it will take for the promised replacement jobs to appear, or what quality of jobs they will be. It could lead to further inequality through divisions into high- and low-paid workers. AI and automation are more likely to threaten workers' rights and solidarity than a BI. However, compared with MTBs, a BI system would provide better protection for the population in the event of either a loss of jobs due to further automation or the recurrence of full employment.

If a BI enables people to have more choice over the

use of their own time, there could be an increase in working on one's own account, such as learning crafts or growing one's own food and selling the surplus. There could be an expansion of true craftsmanship leading to luxury goods that are preferred to robot-designed and created products. There could be an increase in the education, care (especially elder-care), health maintenance, creative and leisure industries. People would make new social alliances for volunteer services and community work.

While not necessarily having a direct effect on environmental issues, it could be enabling by giving individuals the time to reflect and act on them. For example, localisation could reduce both commuting and transport emissions.

11

Evidence from Around the World

AT THE FIRST BI conference in Louvain-La-Neuve, Belgium, in 1986, many delegates presented theoretical research papers. Over the years, their depth and range has increased. They have been accompanied by computer-based, microsimulation thought experiments, and by theoretical papers advising how to conduct BI pilot experiments. Latterly, more empirical evidence from BI experiments has become available.

Both microsimulation and pilot experiments are methods of generating databases that can be subsequently examined. Each has its strengths and weaknesses. Neither can predict the long-term effects of BI systems.

Benefit and taxation microsimulation models are excellent for examining the effects of a new benefit and tax regime on a population sample, identifying who would be better/worse off financially, how many people and by how much. They can calculate the gross and net costs of BI schemes and the values of inequality measures, before and after the changes. On the other hand, they are not good at predicting changes in attitudes or behavioural responses, such as how people will change the use of their time or their consumption patterns as a result of the benefit and tax changes. The costs of setting up and updating a microsimulation model are not cheap, but they are much cheaper than pilot projects.

Several pilot projects based on BI or related concepts have been conducted over the last half century, with interesting results that give indications of attitudinal changes and behavioural responses in a variety of circumstances. However, they are not capable of predicting overall redistribution effects, and there can be ethical implications.

The first of these projects took place in North America: the four Negative Income Tax experiments in the USA between 1968 and 1980; the Mincome Experiment in Dauphin, Manitoba, Canada, 1974–79; and the Alaska Permanent Fund Dividend, 1982–present. Then the focus shifted to Africa and Asia with the project in the rural settlement of Otjivero-Omitara in Namibia, 2008–09; Macau's annual state bonus as part of its Wealth Partaking Scheme, based on gaming profits, 2008–present; Iran, 2010–16; Madhya Pradesh, India, 2011–13. The BI projects came only lately to Europe: Finland, 2017–18.

Other projects have started, or are being planned, in some cities in the Netherlands; in Barcelona, Spain; in Gyeonggi Province in Korea; the short-lived project in Ontario, Canada, 2017–19; in California, USA, by the Y-Combinator company; in Uganda and Kenya (financed privately by charities); and across four local authorities in Scotland. Details can be found on the BIEN website, www.basicincome.org.

Of course, the results of other research projects are also available. These include, for example, research on labour supply models, the effects of poverty and inequality on health and on the life chances of children.

Being long-run projects, several years could elapse before the results of various BI experiments become available. Many BI advocates are confident that sufficient information is already available to enable the effects of BI schemes to be predicted and that a small initial BI could be introduced safely, without waiting for the outcomes of BI experiments.

12

Where Next?

WE LIVE IN times of great uncertainty. Extreme problems face the world, of which the most urgent and severe is still the environmental threat of the climate emergency and species extinction. Only slightly less severe are the lasting effects of the Financial Crisis of 2008–09 and the problems caused by globalisation over the last four decades, which, despite reducing poverty worldwide, has also led to gross inequality of both income and wealth.

The artificial intelligence and automation revolutions have already replaced jobs and lowered wage rates for many employees. The policy of austerity has delayed economic recovery and systematically immiserated the most vulnerable. A BI could help to tackle poverty and inequality and give people more choice in their lives.

However, the urgency of these crises has been overtaken by the outbreak of Covid-19 early in 2020. Never has there been a stronger case for a basic income than this pandemic. If BI systems had already been in place across the world, their populations would have suffered far less anxiety about their subsistence and financial security during the lockdowns.

The virus has revealed the enormous holes in social protection 'safety nets' around the world. Numerous

BIEN-affiliated groups and others have petitioned their governments asking for the immediate implementation of emergency BI schemes during and after the pandemic. Governments have responded with a variety of welcome measures, but few, if any, would be recognised as genuine BIS so far.

On Easter Monday, 13 April 2020, Pope Francis stated: 'Tal vez sea tiempo de pensar en un salario universal...'

As reported by Oxfam on 15 April, this was in the following context:

> Many of you live from day to day, without any type of legal guarantee to protect you. Street vendors, recyclers, carnies, small farmers, construction workers, dressmakers, the different kinds of caregivers: you who are informal, working on your own or in the grassroots economy, you who have no steady income to get you through this hard time... and the lockdowns are becoming unbearable. **This may be the time to consider a universal basic wage** which would acknowledge and dignify the noble, essential tasks you carry out. It would ensure and concretely achieve the ideal, at once so human and so Christian, of no worker without rights. (www.oxfamblogs.org)

A letter, signed by many BI groups, has been sent to António Guterres, UN Secretary General, urging him to invite discussion of, and endorsement for, a BI in the United Nations.

The first duty of each government during the pandemic is to save lives and to minimise the adverse effects of the virus on the physical and mental health of the people.

The second duty must be the security of its population, that is the *income security* of all, providing enough to prevent poverty and for people to feel financially secure. People with mild symptoms would not have to choose between staying at home and working for an income to buy food and pay rent. A BI could have reduced the speed of the spread of the virus. It would have been a public good and helped to protect everyone.

Thirdly, a government must reduce the risk of recession or depression resulting from the reduced spending power of redundant employees and self-employed people. A BI could have maintained income in people's pockets and thus the demand for goods satisfying basic needs. Fewer workers might have been made redundant, and fewer businesses would have been lost. There would have been more surviving companies to pick up renewed demand after the pandemic.

The world will be changed by the pandemic. We will have the opportunity to rethink our priorities. We do not have to return to a business-as-usual, self-serving, exploitative, cruel world that much of it has become. The demonstration of the fact that people do care about their neighbours, even to the extent of putting their lives at risk for them, can be harnessed to create a more compassionate, just world. It could even provide the opportunity to reduce carbon emissions and reverse climate change.

Now is the time of the activist, whose task is to use skills and voice to translate the facts, figures and empirical evidence produced by academics and researchers into narratives and personal stories; to change world views about what is and what could be, and thus to change hearts and minds. Although redistributive policies have occasionally emanated from above, demand for change by a well-informed public, engaging with their elected representatives and briefing them about BI, supported by evidence, so that the representatives can speak confidently on their behalf, would be a much more reliable route.

A basic income is not sufficient on its own for a better society, but it is a necessary condition. It could bring out the best in people, and change societies of fear and despair into ones of compassion, justice, trust and hope. It could lead to new relationships between society, the state and its citizens.

If a few countries implemented BI schemes, and their beneficial effects were obvious, we might see a wave of national BI schemes being adopted worldwide relatively quickly. The next step could be a worldwide BI scheme alongside the national ones, which could help poorer countries and bring about world justice. It could transform societies into ones where everyone matters and all can flourish – a veritable velvet revolution indeed.

13

'Aye, but...'

'NORMATIVE' OBJECTIONS ARE value-based
and merely state a different set of preferences.
Expression of a preference between alternatives is
not necessarily a criticism of the rejected option.
'Positive' criticisms could be tested empirically.
Criticisms of a particular BI proposal or model, even
if justified, cannot necessarily be taken as criticisms
of the generic BI. So, what constitutes valid criticism,
and what is merely a difference of preferences?

In contrast, it would be valid to expose any flaws
discovered in the logic leading to both the outcomes
claimed for BIS, and the mechanisms identified as
the means by which they are brought about. Merely
disagreeing with the outcomes, themselves, is not
a valid criticism. However, proof that *exactly the
same* outcomes could be achieved more efficiently
or effectively by some other method would be valid.
People are also entitled to be wary of unanticipated
consequences.

*So, how can we be sure that a BI scheme will ever
be successfully implemented, given the powerful
political forces that are likely to want to sabotage
it, or to use it as an excuse to dismantle all public
welfare services?*

Our first priority must be to reclaim our democracies, and an informed public must persuade its elected representatives both to implement an appropriate BI system and to protect our public welfare services from sabotage. The first duty of government should be the security of its people – that is, their income security – and not the protection of rich and powerful elites.

Select Bibliography

Bregman, Rutger, *Utopia for Realists: And How We Can Get There*, London: Bloomsbury, 2017

Davala, Sarath, Jhabvala, Renana, Kapoor Mehta, Soumya and Standing, Guy, *Basic Income: A Transformative Policy for India*, London: Bloomsbury, 2015.

Haagh, Louise, *The Case for Universal Basic Income*, Cambridge: Polity Press, 2019

Miller, Annie, *A Basic Income Handbook*, Edinburgh: Luath Press, 2017

Miller, Annie, *A Basic Income Pocketbook*, Edinburgh: Luath Press, 2020

Standing, Guy, *Basic Income: And How We Can Make It Happen*, Basingstoke: Pelican, 2017

Torry, Malcolm, *Why We Need a Citizen's Basic Income: The Desirability, Feasibility and Implementation of an Unconditional Income*, Bristol: Policy Press, 2018

Van Parijs, Philippe and Vanderborght, Yannick, *Basic Income: A Radical Proposal for a Free Society and a Sane Economy*, Cambridge, MA: Harvard University Press, 2017

The following organisations have excellent, informative websites:

The Basic Income Earth Network (BIEN):
www.basicincome.org

The Citizen's Basic Income Trust (CBIT), UK:
www.citizensincome.org

What You Can Do

Donate time, ideas, skills, energy and money to your local BIEN-affiliated organisation.

Become familiar with the arguments for and against basic income, and have some facts and figures about your country at your fingertips.

Use narrative and personal stories to change people's world view about both what is and what could be. Change their hearts and minds.

Discuss the BI idea with your family and friends.

Organise talks, discussions, and debates within your own spheres of influence.

Persuade opinion-formers and policy-makers. Challenge critics.

Discuss basic income with your elected representatives, briefing them so that they are familiar with the idea and confident enough to talk about it in public. Invite them to take part in a debate about basic income. Persuade them to support the idea in their councils or parliaments.

Acknowledgements

AS WITH ALL such endeavours, this book has been written on the shoulders of giants. I must thank past and present trustees of the Citizen's Basic Income Trust and the Citizen's Basic Income Network Scotland. I am also grateful to the friends that I have made through BIEN for stimulating discussions over the last 34 years. The following have made valuable contributions to the clarification of the definition of the generic BI and the development of the related concepts: Hyosang Ahn, Sarath Davala, Ali Mutlu Köylüoglu, Télémaque Masson-Recipon, Guy Standing, Toru Yamamori and Almaz Zelleke. I thank the following for reading and commenting on earlier drafts of this book: John Baker, Coryn Barclay, Mike Danson, Simon Duffy, Jay Ginn, Anne Gray and Jim Pym. I thank Tom Sommerville for the cover photo. Any remaining errors are mine alone. As always, I thank my family and friends for their support and patience, especially Jim and my son, Ben.

A Basic Income Handbook

Annie Miller

ISBN: 978-1-913074-78-6 PBK £12.99

The current social security system is unwieldy,
complex, unjust and unfit for purpose. If we were
designing a system now from scratch for the 21st
century, we would not end up with our present
system. It is a Gordian Knot that cannot be unravelled
or reformed. It must be cut through and replaced by
a system fit for the 21st century. Basic Income is just
such a system. It redefines the relationship between
the state, society and the individual.

This innovative book provides a new perspective
on Basic Income – a regular, unconditional payment
to every individual resident in the country. This
comprehensive book has been rigorously researched
and thus will appeal to academics and policy-makers,
as well as to the general reader who is concerned about
the current state of social security in the UK. Find out
how Basic Income can make a difference to your life.

A Basic Income Pocketbook

Annie Miller

ISBN: 978-1-912147-62-5 PBK £9.99

Rigorously researched and simply explained, this book shows the potential of the Basic Income concept – a regular, unconditional payment to every individual in the country. In a balanced way, it reveals and explains every aspect of the system. More importantly, it shows how the dream of true wellbeing and financial security for all could become a reality.

Luath Press Limited

committed to publishing well written books worth reading

LUATH PRESS takes its name from Robert Burns, whose little collie Luath (*Gael.*, swift or nimble) tripped up Jean Armour at a wedding and gave him the chance to speak to the woman who was to be his wife and the abiding love of his life. Burns called one of the 'Twa Dogs' Luath after Cuchullin's hunting dog in Ossian's *Fingal*. Luath Press was established in 1981 in the heart of Burns country, and is now based a few steps up the road from Burns' first lodgings on Edinburgh's Royal Mile. Luath offers you distinctive writing with a hint of unexpected pleasures.

Most bookshops in the UK, the US, Canada, Australia, New Zealand and parts of Europe, either carry our books in stock or can order them for you. To order direct from us, please send a £sterling cheque, postal order, international money order or your credit card details (number, address of cardholder and expiry date) to us at the address below. Please add post and packing as follows: UK – £1.00 per delivery address; overseas surface mail – £2.50 per delivery address; overseas airmail – £3.50 for the first book to each delivery address, plus £1.00 for each additional book by airmail to the same address. If your order is a gift, we will happily enclose your card or message at no extra charge.

Luath Press Limited

543/2 Castlehill
The Royal Mile
Edinburgh EH1 2ND
Scotland
Telephone: +44 (0)131 225 4326 (24 hours)
email: sales@luath.co.uk
Website: www.luath.co.uk